AF131416

BOOK ANALYSIS

By Jim Hilton

Cat's Cradle

BY KURT VONNEGUT

KURT VONNEGUT

- **Born in Indianapolis, Indiana in 1922.**
- **Died in Manhattan, New York in 2007.**
- **Notable works:**
  - *The Sirens of Titan* (1959), novel
  - *Slaughterhouse-Five* (1969), novel
  - *Breakfast of Champions* (1973), novel

Kurt Vonnegut Jr. was born in Indianapolis, Indiana in 1992. His father Kurt Sr. was an architect, and his mother Edith was from a wealthy brewing family. Vonnegut wrote for and edited student newspapers at high school and Cornell University, where he found writing to be more enjoyable and less stressful than his degree in biochemistry.

Having enlisted in the US army in 1943, he was sent to Europe in late 1944, captured soon after, and lived through the Allied bombing of the German city of Dresden as a prisoner. When he returned home, he married Jane Marie Cox and studied anthropology at the University of Chicago, working as a reporter at night, before becoming a full-time writer in 1952. Vonnegut's early novels were extremely varied in style and content, sometimes containing elements of science fiction, and were moderately successful. He rose to fame when his 1969 novel *Slaughterhouse-Five* became a bestseller. He wrote sporadically for the next decade due to personal difficulties, but then published a series of successful novels through the 1980s and 90s. He died in 2007 in New York.

Today, Vonnegut's work remains extremely popular with the general public and is also widely studied in academic environments. Fellow writers often comment on the ease with which he wrote, despite the fragmented style he employed and the often difficult and painful subjects that he tackled.

CAT'S CRADLE

A ZANY AND EXPERTLY ENTERTAINING YARN ABOUT THE FUTILITY OF MUTUALLY ASSURED DESTRUCTION

- **Genre: novel**
- **Reference edition:** Vonnegut, K. (2011) *Cat's Cradle*. London: Penguin.
- **1st edition:** 1963
- **Themes:** religion, fate, power, technology, the arms race, globalisation

In the late 1940s, Kurt Vonnegut worked in the public relations department of the General Electric research company, where he interviewed scientists about their research methods. The picture he got of men so tied up in the pursuit of knowledge, and so uninterested in the practical applications of their discoveries – in arms development for example – directly influenced his portrayal of the scientist Dr Felix Hoenikker in *Cat's Cradle*: the fictional inventor of the atom bomb.

Like Vonnegut's most famous and celebrated novel, *Slaughterhouse-Five* (1969), *Cat's Cradle* brings together wacky and unorthodox conceits with serious and deeply humanistic explorations of modern history. Vonnegut has an extraordinary ability to tease out the fantastical in the everyday, and to expose the constant absurdity lurking beneath human endeavours: in this case, the build-up of weapons of mass destruction in the Cold War period. At the beginning of the novel, the protagonist and narrator, Jonah, is conducting research for a book about the atom-bombing of Hiroshima. But soon he begins to hear rumours about an even deadlier weapon called *ice-nine*: the final, cursed invention of the genius and sociopathic scientist Dr Felix Hoenikker. The fatal substance is split equally between Hoenikker's three children, Newt, Angela and Frank, all three of them misfits, and all equally unfit for the great responsibility incumbent on them. Over 50 years on, with our increasingly advanced military technology and capability, Vonnegut's satire of political myopia and grandiose human folly is unfortunately as relevant and pressing as ever.

SUMMARY

The narrator, Jonah, introduces himself and explains some tenets of the Bokononist religion: "We Bokononists believe that humanity is organized into teams, teams that do God's will without ever discovering what they are doing. Such a team is called a *karass*" (p. 2). Over the course of the novel, Jonah will recount the fate of his *karass*. Once upon a time, we are told, Jonah was writing a book about the bombing of Hiroshima called *The Day the World Ended*. For the purposes of research, he wrote to Newton Hoenikker – one of the three children of Dr Felix Hoenikker, the late inventor of the atomic bomb. Newt writes back, telling Jonah that on the day the bomb was dropped, his father Felix Hoenikker was playing cat's cradle with a piece of string. Soon after this correspondence, Jonah reads in the paper that Newt has just had a flash in the pan affair with a Ukrainian dancer called Zinka – who briefly defected from the USSR, before changing her mind and returning home.

Jonah, meanwhile, books a meeting with the Vice-president of the Research Laboratory at the General Forge and Foundry Company, where Felix Hoenikker used to work. Arriving in Ilium, Jonah spends an evening in the hotel bar, where he gets drunk with the locals, and as a result is badly hungover for his meeting the next morning. Dr Asa Breed, the Vice-president, drives Jonah to the Laboratory and tells him a little about Felix and Felix's wife Emily. Jonah manages to annoy Dr Breed with the manner of his questions, and Dr Breed staunchly defends the value of "pure research" (p. 29). He describes to Jonah the concept of *ice-nine* – a molecular rearrangement of frozen water with a melting point of 130 degrees Fahrenheit which, if it touched the ocean, would be capable of freezing all the water on earth. According to Dr Breed, this was one of Felix Hoenikker's last conceptual achievements, although one he never put into action. Here Jonah wades into the story with his narrative foreknowledge and tells the reader that in fact, Felix Hoenikker did invent *ice-nine* before his death, and the small sample had been divided up by his three children.

After visiting the Laboratory, Jonah goes to see Felix Hoenniker's tomb in the local graveyard. The taxi driver points him to a massive alabaster phallus, but when Jonah reads the inscription, he realises it is actually the tomb of Felix's wife Emily, erected by the three children. Jonah goes into a tombstone showroom across the road and speaks to the owner, Marvin Breed, brother of Dr Asa Breed, who tells him that Emily Hoenikker was the most beautiful woman in Ilium and that Felix did not deserve her. On the way back to his hotel, Jonah stops at Jack's Hobby Shop, where the other Hoenikker son, Frank – widely believed to be dead – used to work. The owner, Jack, takes him into the basement and shows him the extraordinary model layout that Frank created, and mourns him as a lost genius.

After returning home to New York, Jonah comes across a special supplement in the *Sunday Times* dedicated to the tiny island Republic of San Lorenzo. Inside he finds a picture of the Republic's dictator, "Papa" Monzano, and another picture of "a narrow-shouldered, fox-faced, immature young man", "identified as Major General Franklin Hoenikker, *Minister* of *Science and Progress in the Republic of San Lorenzo*" (p. 57). Coincidentally, Jonah receives a magazine assignment to go to San Lorenzo and write a story on a former sugar magnate, Julian Castle, who now runs a free hospital called "the House of Hope and Mercy in the Jungle" (p. 60).

On the plane to San Lorenzo, Jonah meets Horlick and Claire Minton – the former of whom is the new American ambassador – and H. Lowe Crosby, a bicycle manufacturer from Chicago, and his wife Hazel. Crosby fills in some details about San Lorenzo, including that all crimes are punishable by being hung on a great metal hook. Jonah borrows a copy of a book titled *San Lorenzo: The Land, the History, the People* from the Mintons, and written by Julian Castle's son Philip. He reads about Bokonon, born Lionel Boyd Johnson, and his Odyssean wanderings from country to country and coast to coast, before finally being chased by a gale onto San Lorenzo, along with an "idealistic Marine deserter, Earl McCabe" (p. 76).

At a stopover in Puerto Rico, Newt and Angela Hoenikker board the plane, and Jonah goes to talk with them. Angela tells him about the day their father died – a Christmas Eve at their beach house. She also shows him a photo of her husband, Harrison C. Connors, a handsome man and the president of Fabri-Tek. Jonah returns to reading his book and reads about the mysterious island beauty, Mona Aamons Monzano – the adopted daughter of "Papa" Monzano. He also reads about how Bokonon and McCabe quickly took charge of the struggling Republic: how McCabe and his second in command, Monzano, took over the matters of government, and Bokonon set about making his own religion.

The plane lands in San Lorenzo, and the travellers are given a welcoming ceremony by "Papa" Monzano. Jonah sees signs forbidding in no uncertain terms any practising of Bokononism. There is a large crowd and Frank Hoenikker and Mona Aamons Monzano are also in attendance. Towards the end of his address, "Papa" Monzano collapses with chest pain and must be taken away. Jonah and the Crosbys go their hotel, which is owned by Philip Castle, and Jonah meets him in the foyer, where he is completing a mosaic of Mona. While at the hotel, Jonah also spots two workmen engaged in what seems to be a

Bokononist ritual, and, terrified, they swear him to secrecy. Jonah then gets a telephone call from Frank Hoenikker, who tells him urgently to come over to his house.

Arriving at Frank's, Jonah finds Newt, Angela and Julian Castle but no Frank. Julian tells Jonah more about the history of Bokononism: it was actually Bokonon's own idea for his religion to be outlawed, "in order to give the religious life of the people more zest, more tang" (p. 123). The administration's war against Bokononism is a kind of lie, as Monzano knows all too well that his power depends on its permanent state of fierce opposition to Bokononism. Julian Castle reveals that he himself is a Bokononist. Later that evening, there is an island-wide blackout, and finally Frank appears and asks to speak with Jonah privately. Frank confesses that he prefers to work behind the scenes: he is "no good at facing the public", and therefore unfit to become the next president (p. 142). Frank asks Jonah if he would take the job, and as part of it, marry the beautiful Mona Aamons Monzano. Jonah, at first astounded, finally accepts, and is given an audience with Mona, where he performs his first Bokononist ritual: the *boko-maru*.

Frank and Jonah drive out to Monzano's castle to obtain the dying president's blessing. They find Monzano in a bed "made of a golden dinghy – tiller, painter, oarlocks and all, all gilt", which was the very boat in which Bokonon and McCabe first landed on San Lorenzo (p. 155). Around the sick man's neck is a "chain with a cylinder the size of a rifle cartridge for a pendant" (*ibid*.). Monzano charges Jonah with finding and killing Bokonon, before demanding – with everyone present – to have his own Bokononist last rites.

The next day is the Day of the Hundred Martyrs to Democracy, and also Jonah's swearing-in ceremony. He writes a speech in which he decides for the good of all to continue the government's longstanding policy outlawing Bokononism: "good and evil had to remain separate; good in the jungle, and evil in the palace" (p. 162). The Hoenikkers, Mona, Julian and Philip Castle, the Mintons and the Crosbys are all assembled on the castle battlements for the festivities – although only Frank and Mona know about Jonah's appointment. One of the hors d'oeuvres violently disagrees with Jonah and he goes to the bathroom. On coming out, he finds Monzano's doctor, who informs him that Monzano has died and is frozen completely stiff. They go into the room together and Jonah finds Monzano frozen in his ghastly death pose, with the little cylinder uncapped and held to his mouth. The doctor, who has traces of *ice-nine* on his hands, attempts to wash them in a basin of water and freezes to death himself. Jonah quickly sends for the three Hoenikker children, who admit to their shared ownership of the deadly substance – and Frank admits to giving a portion to Monzano. They tell Jonah about the night of their father's death: how he left a saucepan of *ice-nine* in the kitchen, meaning to melt it down again to water, just before he died. The four of them set about disinfecting the room of *ice-nine* with a broom and blow-torch, before sealing up the room and returning to the celebration upstairs.

The air show begins as six fighter planes make their pass over the castle. One of them is trailing smoke, however, and suddenly falls from the sky, crashing into the cliffs below and exploding, which sets off a series of rockslides. The foundations of the castle begin to collapse and the two Mintons are lost as the battlement where they are standing falls away into the sea. Below, in the now exposed belly of the castle, Jonah watches as the golden dinghy containing the frozen dead Monzano slowly teeters and falls into the sea, immediately turning the entire ocean and all the world's water into *ice-nine*. The sky is suddenly wracked with dreadful tornadoes, tearing at the land, and Jonah and Mona flee for shelter in the castle's underground dungeon.

They hide out for a week, as the tornadoes die down, and Jonah reads through *The Books of Bokonon*. Once out in the open, the pair discover a vast crowd of frozen, dead San Lorenzans, and on a boulder nearby, a note written and signed by Bokonon. The holy man confesses to having instructed the crowd to kill themselves, and before Jonah can stop her, Mona quickly follows suit.

Jonah miraculously bumps into another troupe of survivors, the Crosbys, Frank and Newt, and the five of them set up a strange communal life together, living off whatever food they can scavenge or defrost. Six months later, Newt and Jonah are driving into San Lorenzo's capital to obtain some paints, when they spot Bokonon through the window. Jonah gets out of the car and approaches him, and asks: "May I ask what you're thinking?" (p. 205). Bokonon responds that he has been trying to think of the final sentence for *The Books of Bokonon*, and he hands it to Jonah on a piece of paper:

> "If I were a younger man, I would write a history of human stupidity; and I would climb to the top of Mount McCabe and lie down on my back with my history for a pillow; and I would take from the ground some of the blue-white poison that makes statues of men; and I would make a statue of myself, lying on my back, grinning horribly, and thumbing my nose at You Know Who" (p. 206)

CHARACTER STUDY

JONAH

Jonah's self-introduction at the novel's opening, "Call me Jonah" (p. 1), directly recalls the famous opening line of Herman Melville's (American writer, 1819-1891) great American epic, *Moby Dick*. Like Melville's protagonist, Ishmael, Jonah is in some ways the main character: we see through his eyes, and yet he occasionally feels almost exterior to the action. Events and characters coalesce around him and he just about manages to keep up. He is Vonnegut's American everyman: good-natured, dry-witted and highly curious about the world around him.

DR FELIX HOENIKKER

The scientist and inventor of the atom bomb, Dr Felix Hoenikker is dead before the action of the novel begins, and yet he nonetheless becomes one of Vonnegut's central characters. The plot is really a tracing of the elaborate fallout of his final invention: the deadly molecular rearrangement of water, *ice-nine*. Vonnegut presents him as a child-like genius with an incredible mind for understanding the physical nature and laws of the universe, but a total indifference to human affairs, morality, politics and even family.

NEWT HOENIKKER

Newt Hoenikker is the youngest of Dr Felix Hoenikker's children and apparently the most well-adjusted of them. He is also a little person, and unfortunately Vonnegut has occasional recourse to poking fun at the condition. But on the whole, Newt's portrayal is positive and three-dimensional. He is artistic, serious-minded, and patient towards his older sister Angela and her often stifling attempts to mother him.

ANGELA HOENIKKER

Angela is not an entirely sympathetic character, at least through Jonah's eyes. But she is clearly the victim of her father's dereliction of familial duty, while also being the most openly devoted to his memory. When her mother, Emily Hoenikker, died, Angela as the oldest child was left to care for her younger brothers, as well as for her child-like father. This left her with little time to attend to herself, and her only outlet was the clarinet, on which she is extraordinarily gifted. One wonders what she could have made of herself had she been granted a real childhood.

FRANK HOENIKKER

Frank is the middle child and the one most obviously like his father. He is self-confessedly not a people person. He has a great technical mind, but not one sensitive to those around him, nor to the social or even spiritual implications of his decisions. His gift of *ice-nine* to the dictator "Papa" Monzano is ultimately responsible for freezing all the water on Earth; yet Vonnegut gives us reason to believe that such an event would have happened anyway.

ANALYSIS

The 1960s was a tumultuous decade in the West, and especially in the United States. In November 1963, the year Kurt Vonnegut published *Cat's Cradle,* John F. Kennedy (American President, 1917-1963) was assassinated in Dallas, Texas. Numerous high-profile assassinations would continue to mar the fabric of American political life throughout the decade. African-American leaders Malcolm X (American minister and activist, 1925-1965) and Martin Luther King Jr. (American minister and activist, 1929-1968) were shot dead in 1965 and 1968 respectively, while John F. Kennedy's brother, Robert F. Kennedy (American politician, 1925-1968), would also be shot and killed in 1968. While racial tensions flared up across the country, with more and more African-Americans demanding equal rights, from 1965 onwards, America also found itself involved in a calamitous and unwinnable war against the Communists in Vietnam. This highly unpopular conflict fed into discontent at home, and a burgeoning anti-war movement among students and activists initiated large-scale protests, which in turn provoked harsh crackdowns by the government and police. In 1970 at Kent State University, four American students were killed when Ohio Guardsmen fired into a crowd of unarmed protestors.

Such upheaval had a direct effect on, and was directly affected by, contemporary cultural production. Artists, musicians, writers and filmmakers politicised their work, pitting it against the authoritarian and imperial structures of American power in the post-war period, and by 1968 Theodore Roszak (American academic, 1933-2011) identified what he called the *counterculture*. The leading cultural movements of the day did not express or represent the accepted and enforced rules of society, but violently challenged them. Culture and society at large were in fierce conflict.

Cat's Cradle is a novel at the forefront of this developing mode. Vonnegut's treatment of American social mores is ingeniously satirical and irreverent, as is his use of genre: he blurs the historical and the fantastical, the literary and the nonsensical. Humour is his weapon, and the stings of his critique are hidden and nested in the sheer warmth and joviality of his voice. He intones his gravely pessimistic vision of human annihilation with an infectious optimism – a sort of gentle stupidity which is made to feel like a quality aiding survival in the absurd conditions of the Cold War world.

In his book, *The Making of a Counter Culture* (1969), Theodore Roszak identified the main target of the youthful countercultural movements as *technocracy*. Rather than adhering to a binary of Capitalism or Communism, this political, institutional development crossed the East-West divide and was as rampant in the USSR. as it was in America. It was a mode of organisation that privileged expertise, administration and the bureaucratic division of labour. Under technocracy, the world is understood as a kind of machine that can reach a state of maximum efficiency through careful calculation and planning. In *Cat's Cradle*, the vice-president of the General Forge and Foundry Research Laboratory, Dr Asa

Breed, views scientific knowledge as a quantifiable resource. He calls it "the most valuable commodity on earth", and claims that "The more truth we have to work with, the richer we become" (p. 29). Such a statement blatantly ignores the important question: is the desire for wealth a good reason to do something? But for scientists such as Dr Breed, such moral questions have no real existence: they cannot be measured on a graph or seen under a microscope, so they are not there. Speaking to Jonah, Dr Breed's secretary recalls an instance when she expressed the sentiment to Dr Felix Hoenikker that "God is love"; his response was "What is God? What is love?" (p. 39).

REVISING THE SECOND WORLD WAR

Cat's Cradle is one of several important American novels that, from the 1960s onwards, began to revise and interrogate the role the United States played in the Second World War. In 1961, Joseph Heller (American writer, 1923-1999) published his blistering tragi-comic novel, *Catch-22*, about a bomber squadron stationed in Italy, while in 1973, Thomas Pynchon (American writer, born in 1937) published his epic World War II saga, *Gravity's Rainbow*. Kurt Vonnegut would finally establish his reputation as a writer with his novel *Slaughterhouse-Five* (1969), which mingled time-travel quirkiness with Vonnegut's own experiences as a prisoner of war in Dresden, Germany during the infamous air-bombing of the city.

The euphoria and relief over the defeat of Japan and the Nazis, and the industriousness of post-war planning and development in Europe and in South-East Asia permeated American society through the 1940s and 1950s. The country entered a phase of vast economic expansion: the consumer economy was growing and America was exporting its products and fashions all over the world. Modern middle-class life as we know it was developing in homes across America, as white goods and cars became realistically affordable.

But all through this period, the Holocaust cast its enormous shadow over the Western world. As the scale of the atrocity became clearer, so it became less and less comprehensible. How could one of the most developed and supposedly civilised countries in the world commit such an act of murderous horror against its own people? Theodor Adorno (German philosopher, 1903-1969) famously declared that there could be no poetry after Auschwitz. On the one hand, the Holocaust confirmed the Nazi regime as being among the most evil in recorded history, and in that way further vindicated the Allied war effort. On the other, it threw a ray of doubt over the whole supposed project of Western culture and civilisation. On the Allied side, how could Americans square the carpet-bombing of Tokyo and the atomic bombs dropped on Hiroshima and Nagasaki with America's public ideology of freedom and democracy for all? In these cities and in German cities like Dresden, the Allied forces intentionally targeted and killed hundreds of thousands of innocent civilians. The Western powers advertised themselves as the defenders of the innocent; entirely unlike the Nazis who had not even a passing respect for human life. The uncomfortable truth was that the Allies were in fact less distinct from the Nazis than they thought.

Novels like *Catch-22, Cat's Cradle* and *Slaughterhouse-Five* began to address the matter of American barbarity in the Second World War. They did not present the United States' military campaign as a force of righteous good in the world, but rather as a bungling and myopic operation overseen by petulant windbags. In *Cat's Cradle*, the development of apocalyptic weapons is presented as the childish, unworldly obsession of a scientist whose office is full of cheap knick-knacks and who may as well be a child: a genius, but one whose gift has no meaningful or willed connection to the world. Dr Felix Hoenikker is a man completely unburdened by responsibility: a careless husband, a careless father and a careless human, blissfully unconcerned by the radical fallout his inventions may entail for the human race. Vonnegut's imagined landscape at the end of the novel, in which all the world's water has been frozen into *ice-nine*, is a fictive one. But the threat of a post-atomic landscape was very real at the time, and remains real now, as the world's superpowers continue to hold onto nuclear weapons. Such a landscape was a historical actuality in the Second World War, and the perpetrator was of course the United States. *Cat's Cradle* is, in a way, Vonnegut's own refracted record of the bombing of Hiroshima.

FURTHER REFLECTION

SOME QUESTIONS TO THINK ABOUT...

- As a mainstay of genre fiction, science-fiction is viewed by many as an antithesis to serious literature. How might *Cat's Cradle* refute this opinion?
- *Cat's Cradle* is organized into 127 very short chapters, each with its own title. Why might Kurt Vonnegut have chosen to set out his novel in this way?
- The first line of *Cat's Cradle* directly recalls the opening of Herman Melville's *Moby Dick*. Why might Vonnegut want to reference Melville's work here?
- Throughout the novel, Vonnegut makes frequent use of his invented Bokononist vocabulary. What is your personal response to these invented words? Do you find them funny/insightful/distracting?
- The second part of the story takes place in the fictional Republic of San Lorenzo. What kind of geo-political relationship does Vonnegut

represent as existing between the United States and emerging states in South and Central America?

- In your opinion, does Vonnegut succeed in balancing seriousness and comedy in *Cat's Cradle*? Why/why not?
- In your opinion, what is the symbolic or metaphorical significance of the oft-referenced figure of the cat's cradle in the novel?

We want to hear from you!
Leave a comment on your online library
and share your favourite books on social media!

FURTHER READING

REFERENCE EDITION

- Vonnegut, K. (2011) *Cat's Cradle.* London: Penguin.

MORE FROM BRIGHTSUMMARIES.COM

- Reading guide – *Slaughterhouse-Five* by Kurt Vonnegut.

www.brightsummaries.com

Ebook EAN: 9782808019767

Paperback EAN: 9782808019774

Legal Deposit: D/2019/12603/155

Cover: © Primento

Digital conception by Primento, the digital partner of
publishers.

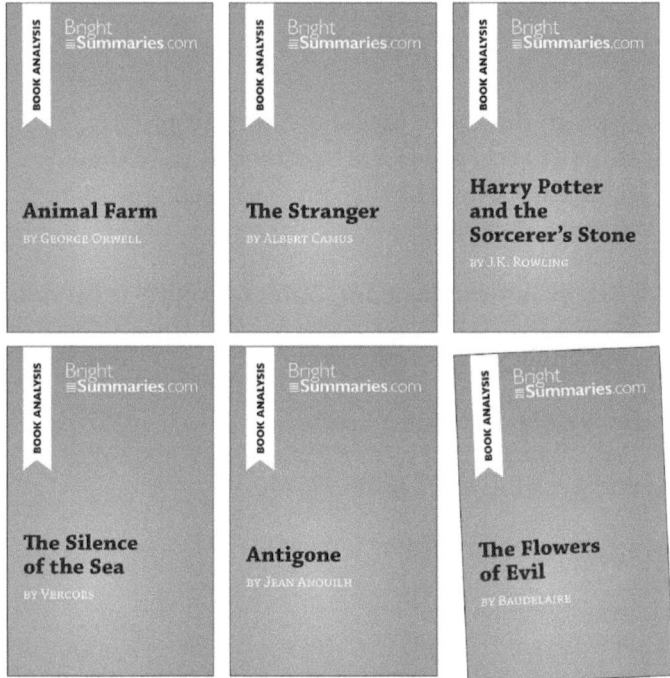